MW00390196

Architect Houses

Coloring Book

Detailed & Relaxing! Exterior Design Houses, Buildings Architecture Designs - Real Estate Drawings to Color

Rachel Mintz

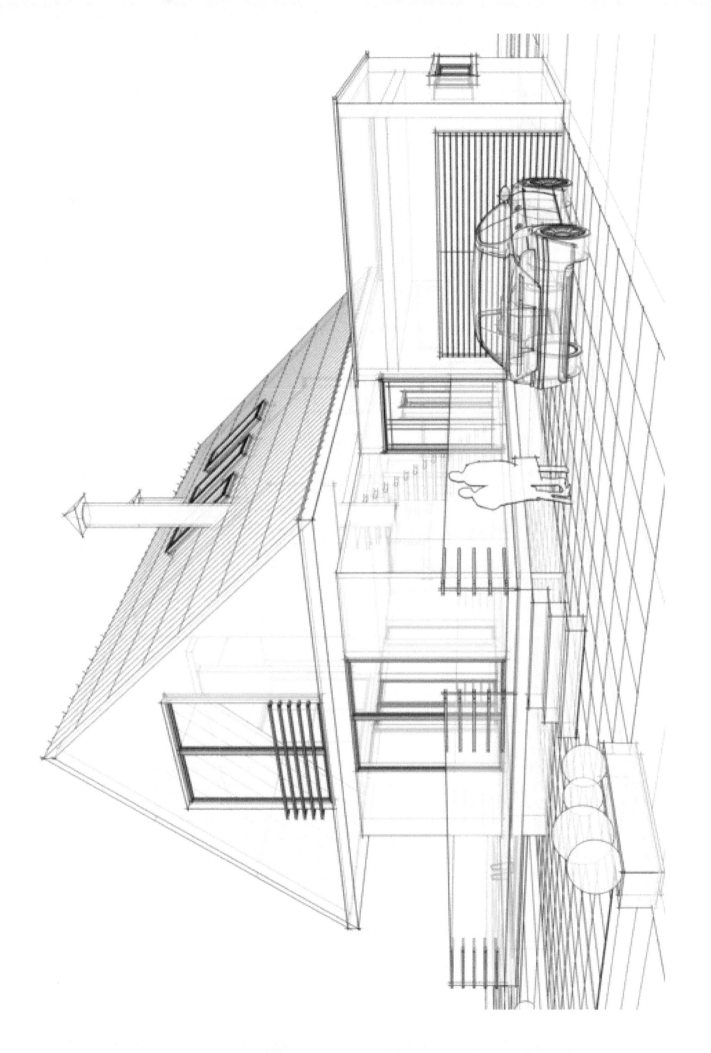

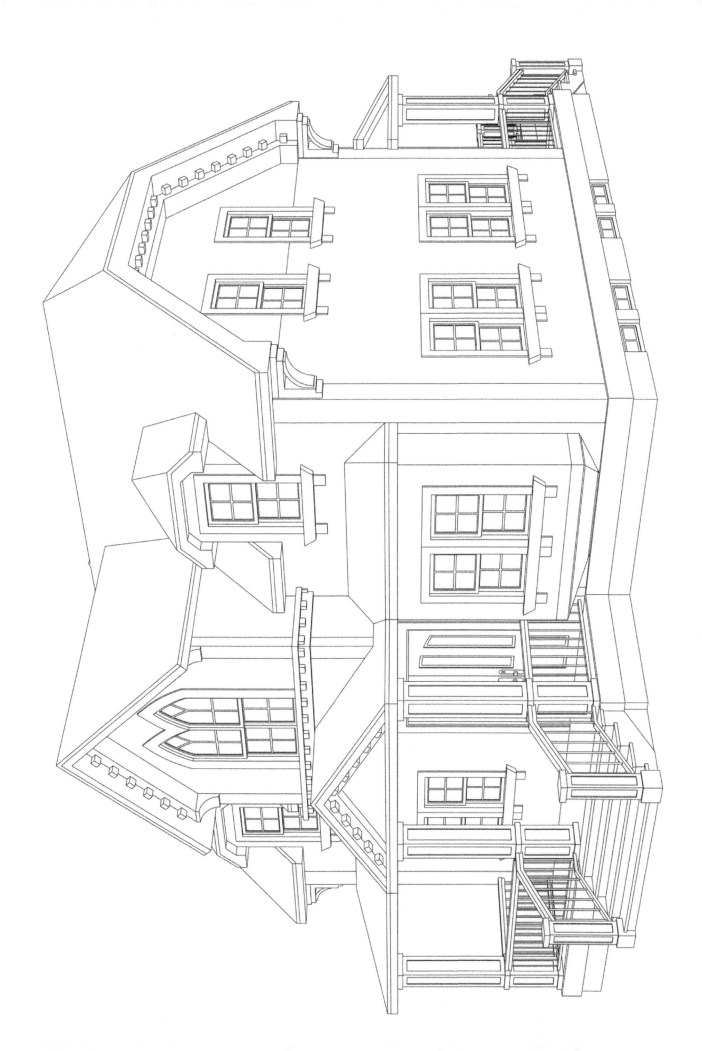

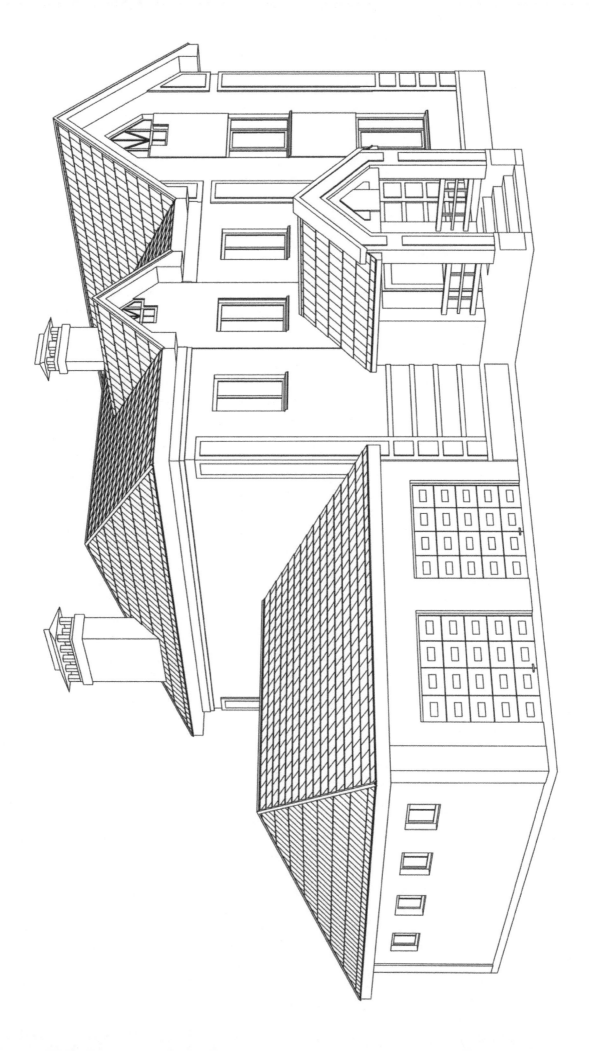

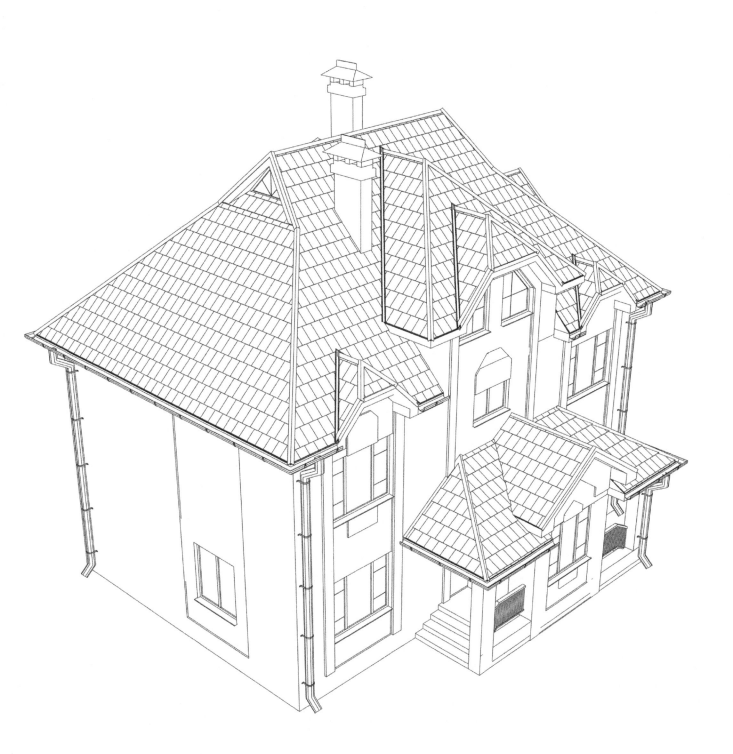

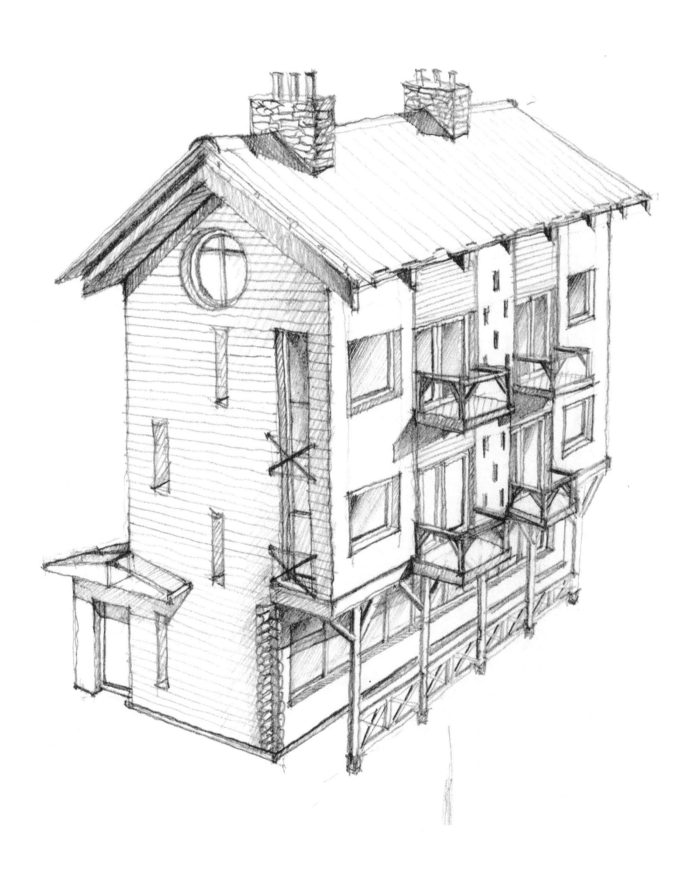

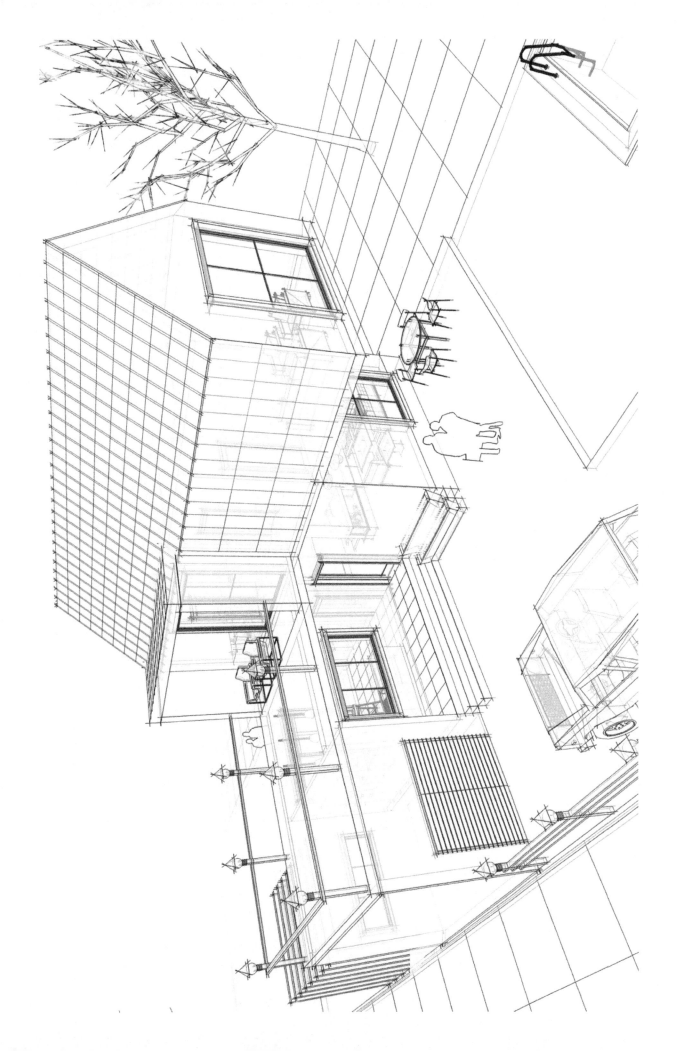

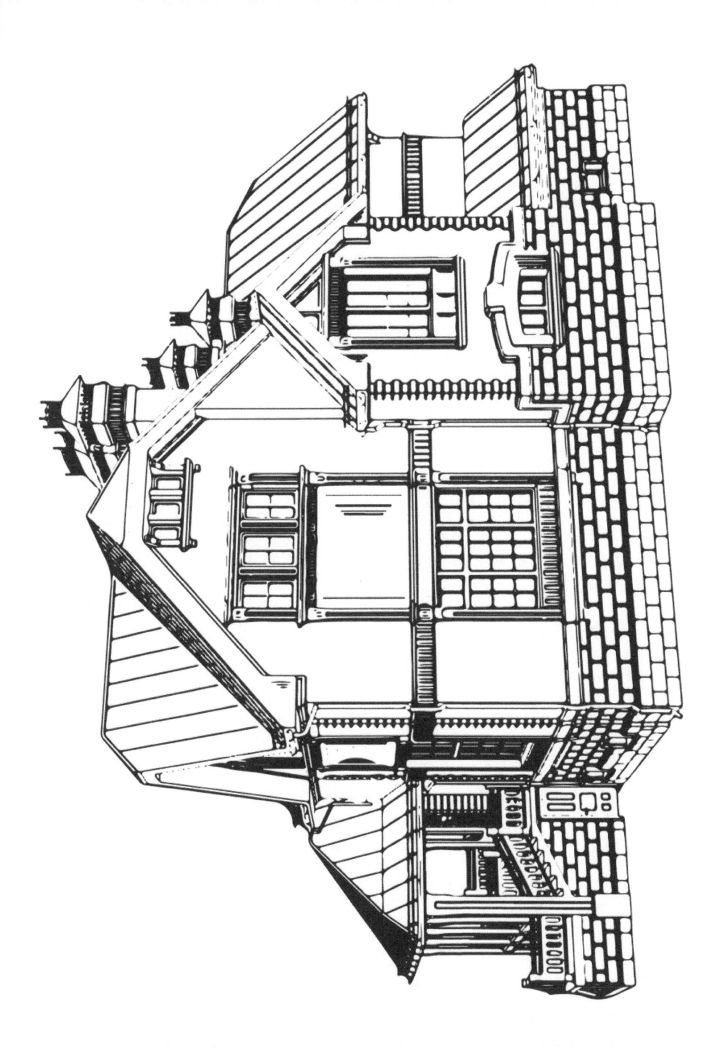

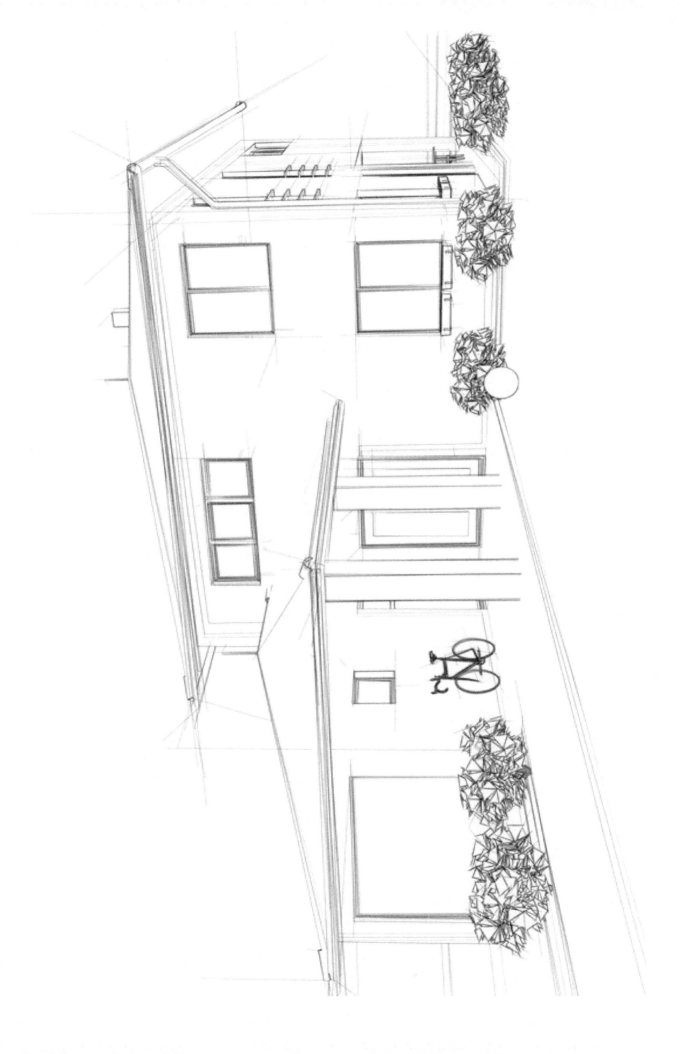

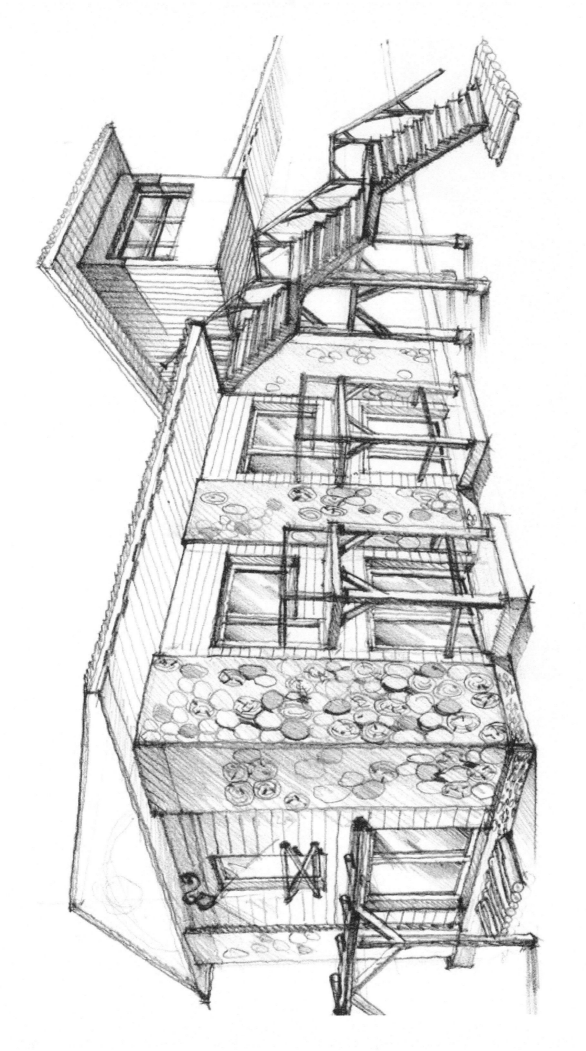

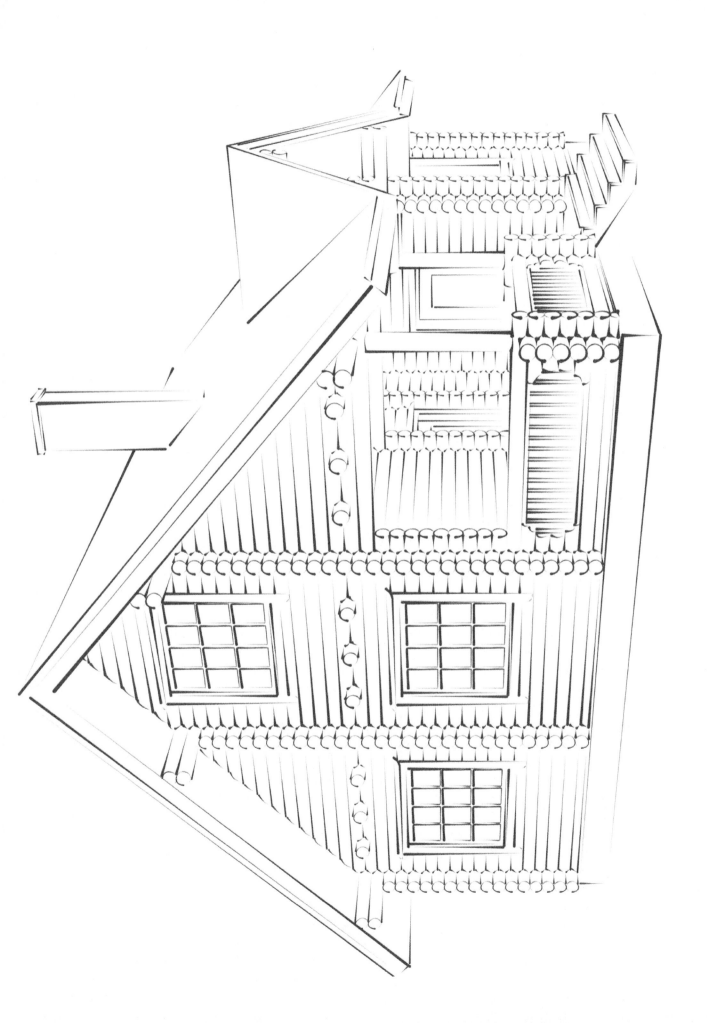

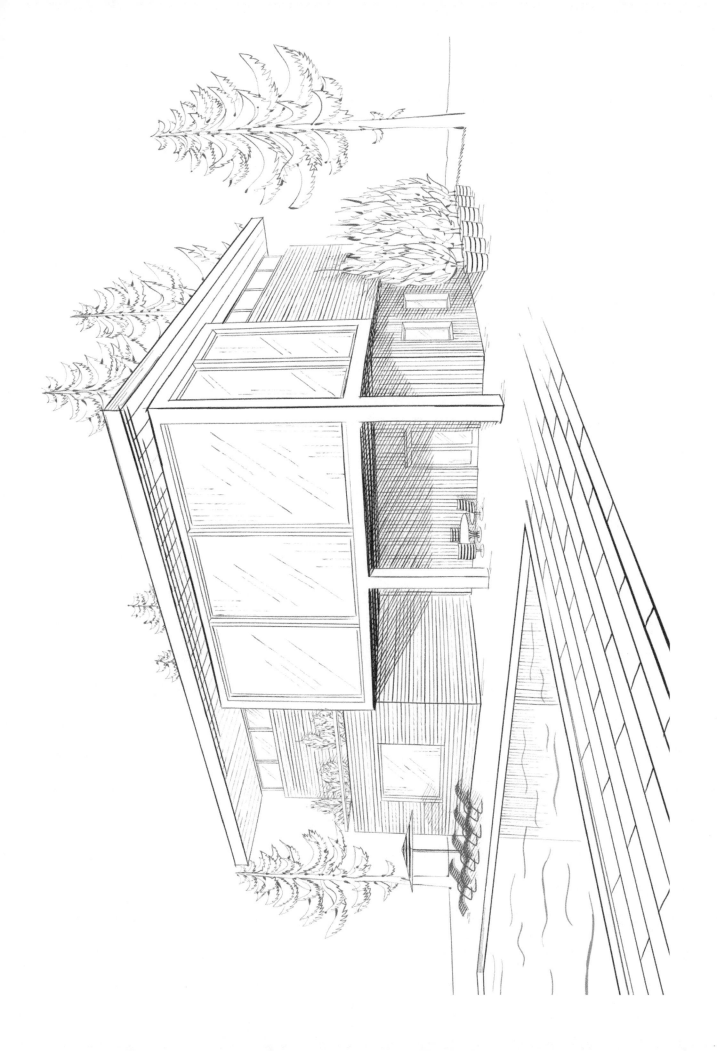

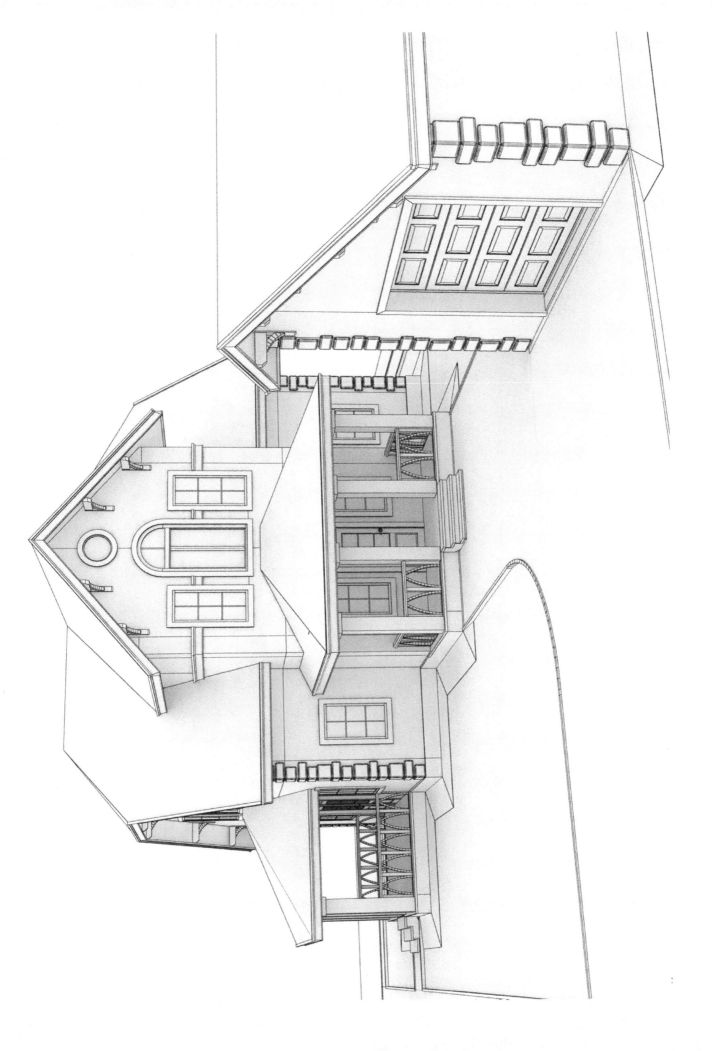

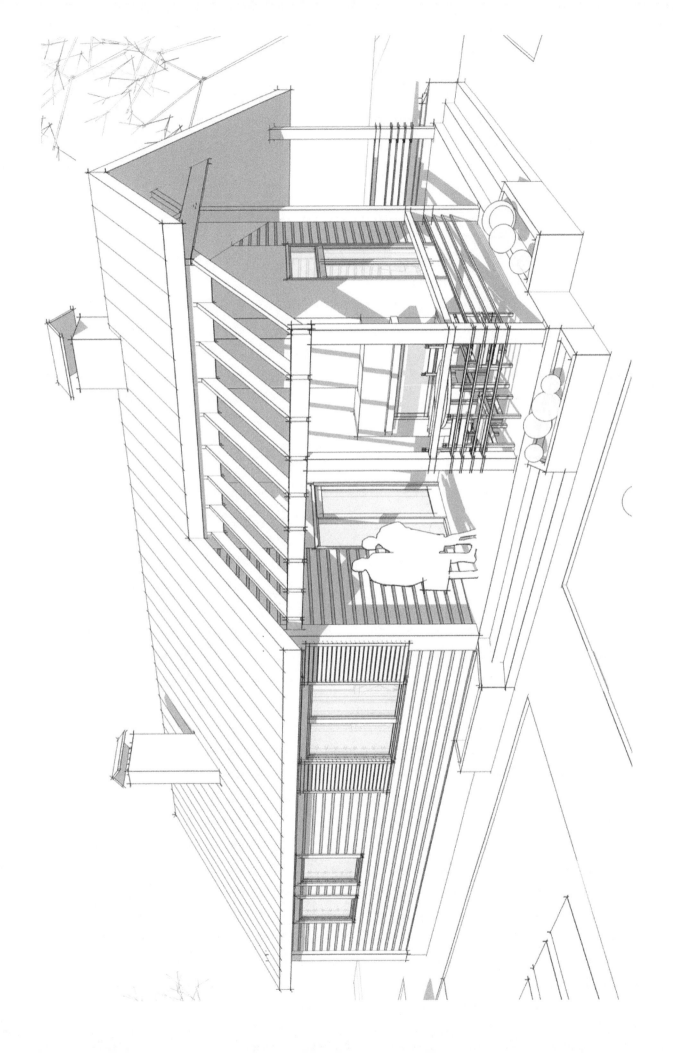

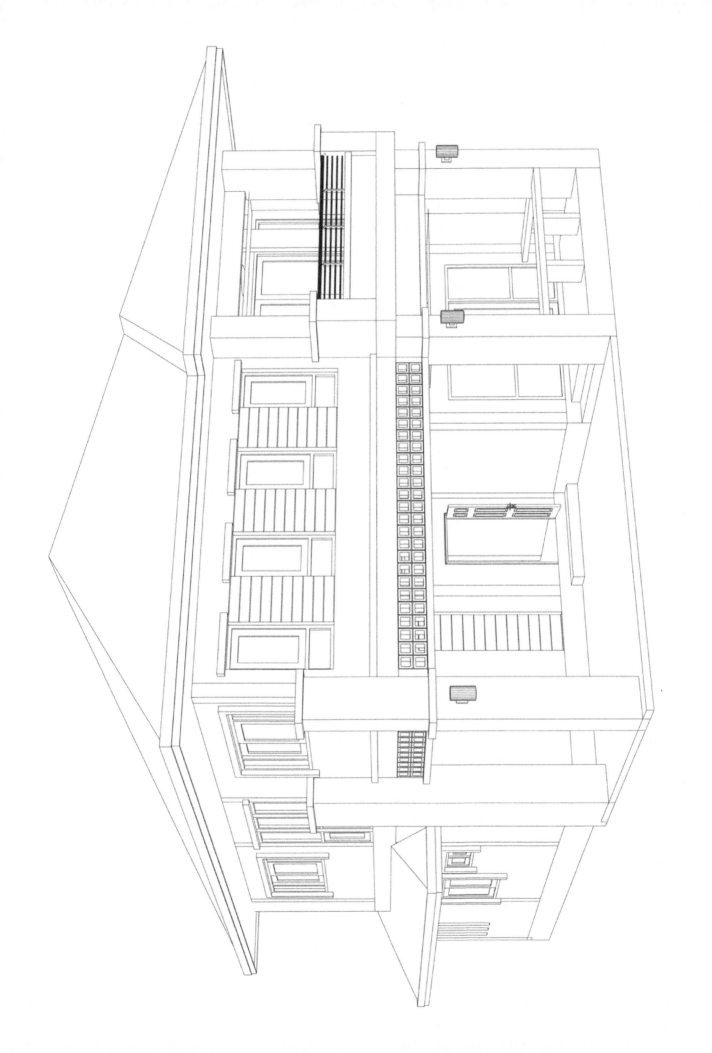

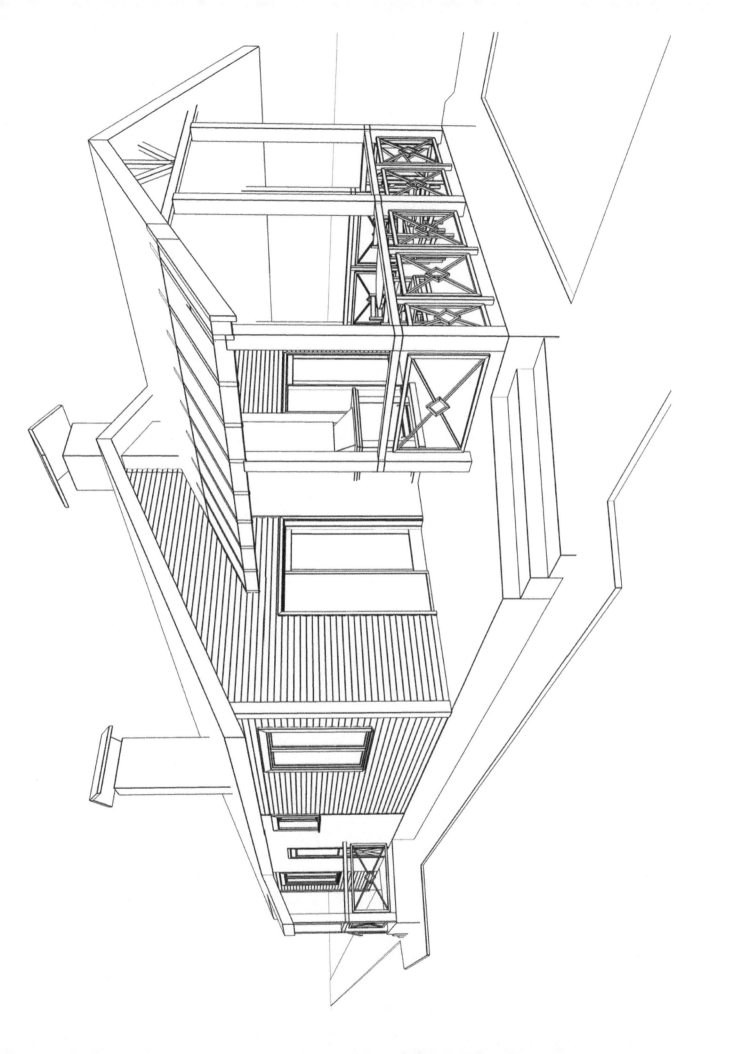

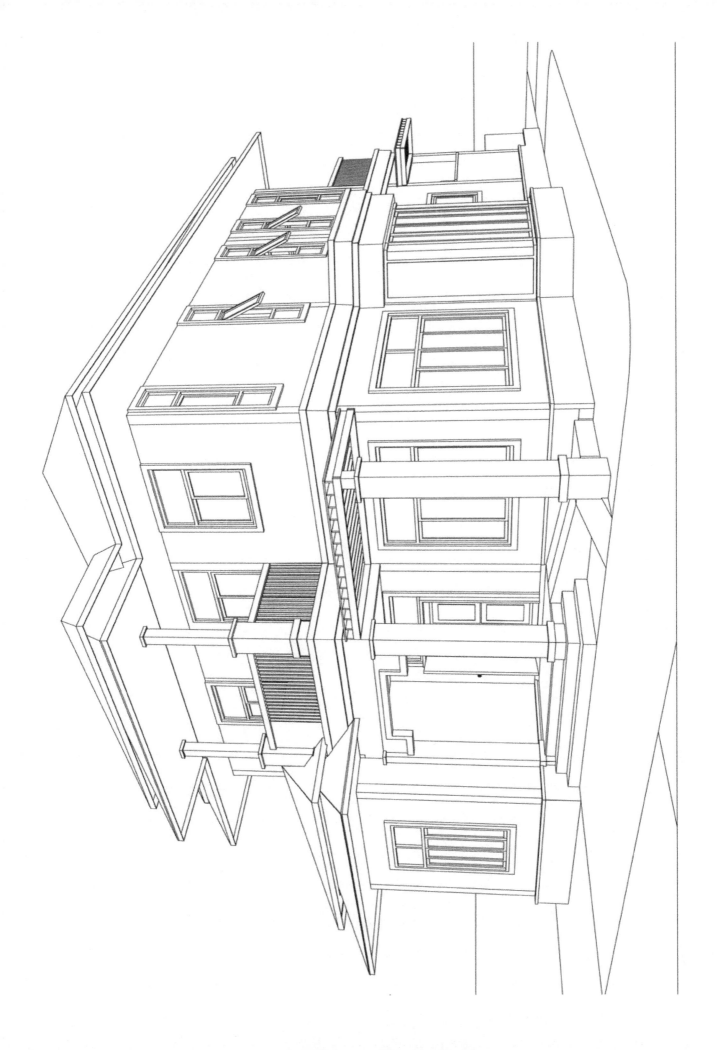

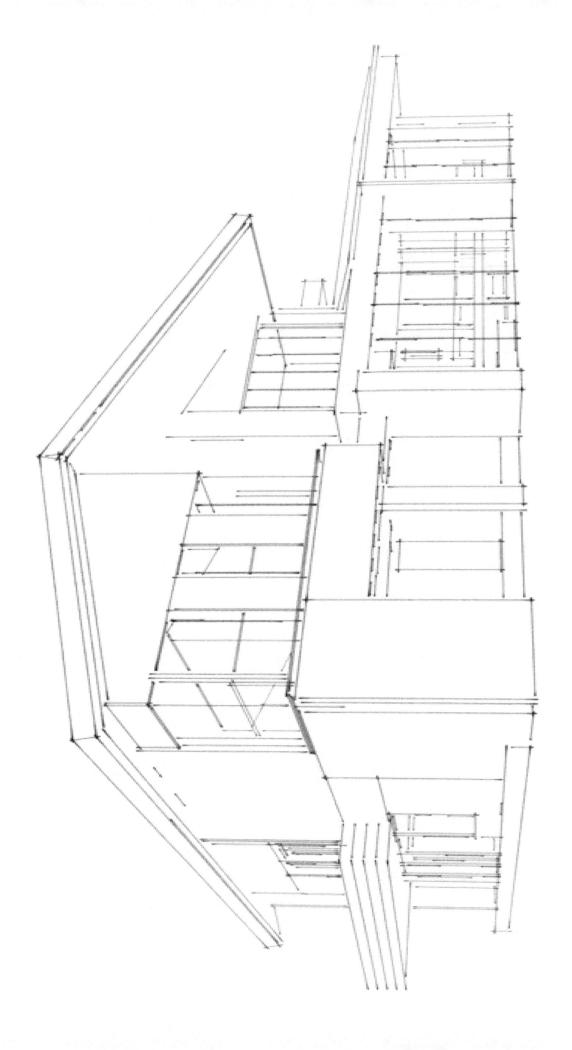

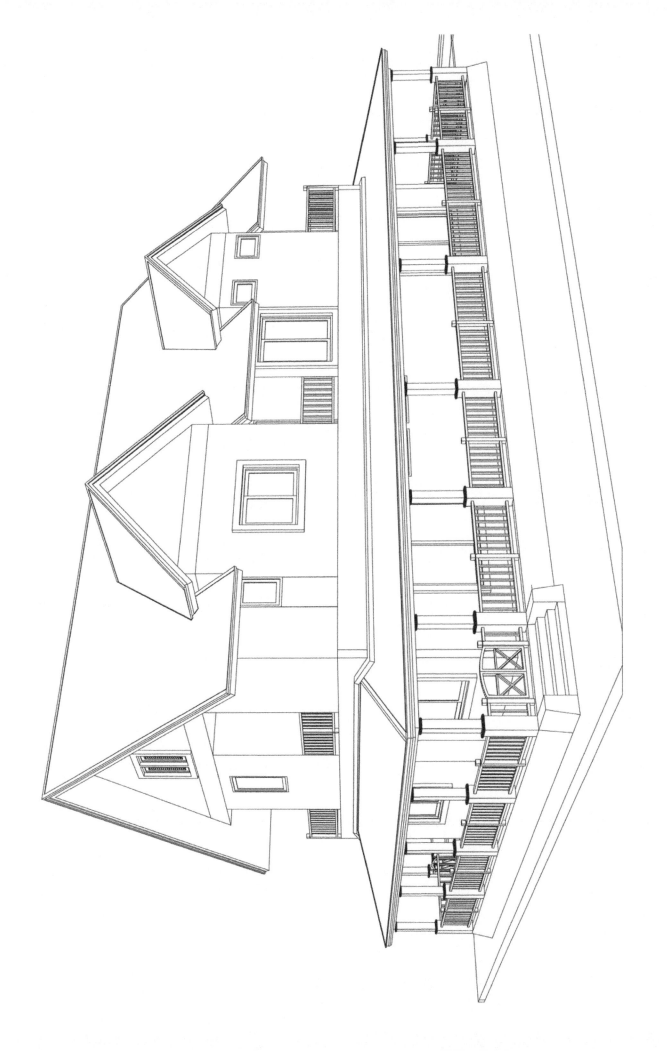

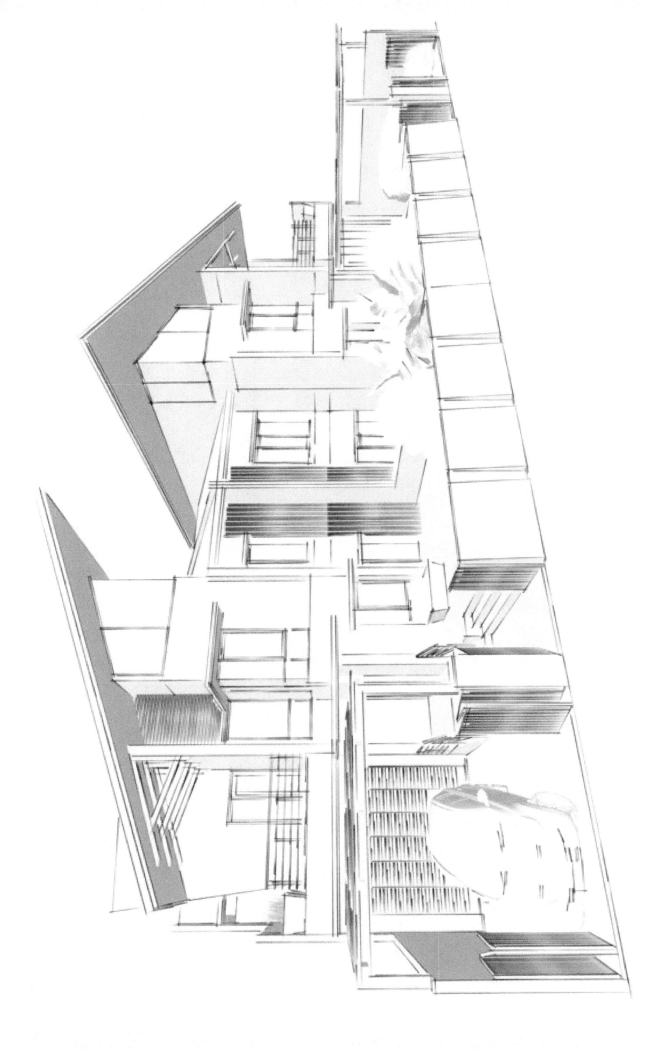

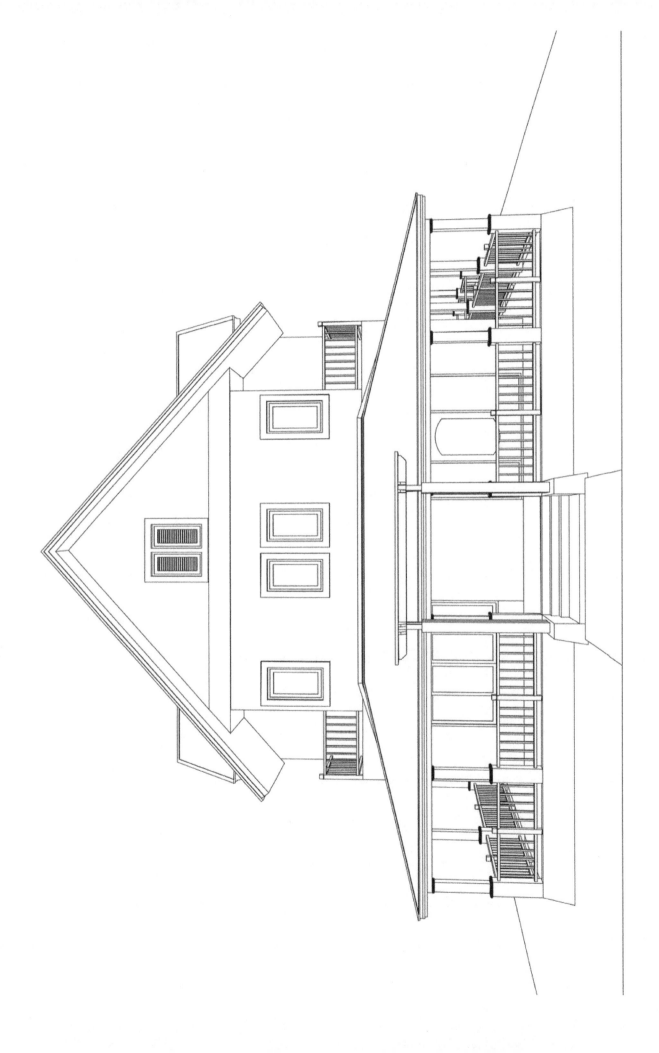

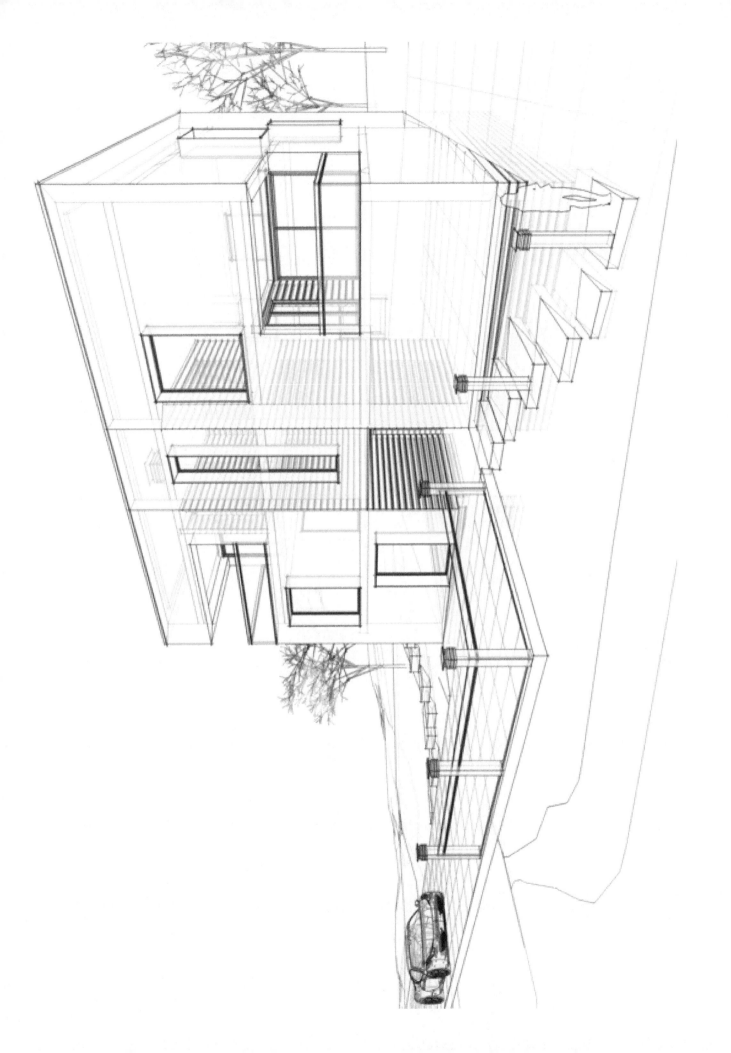

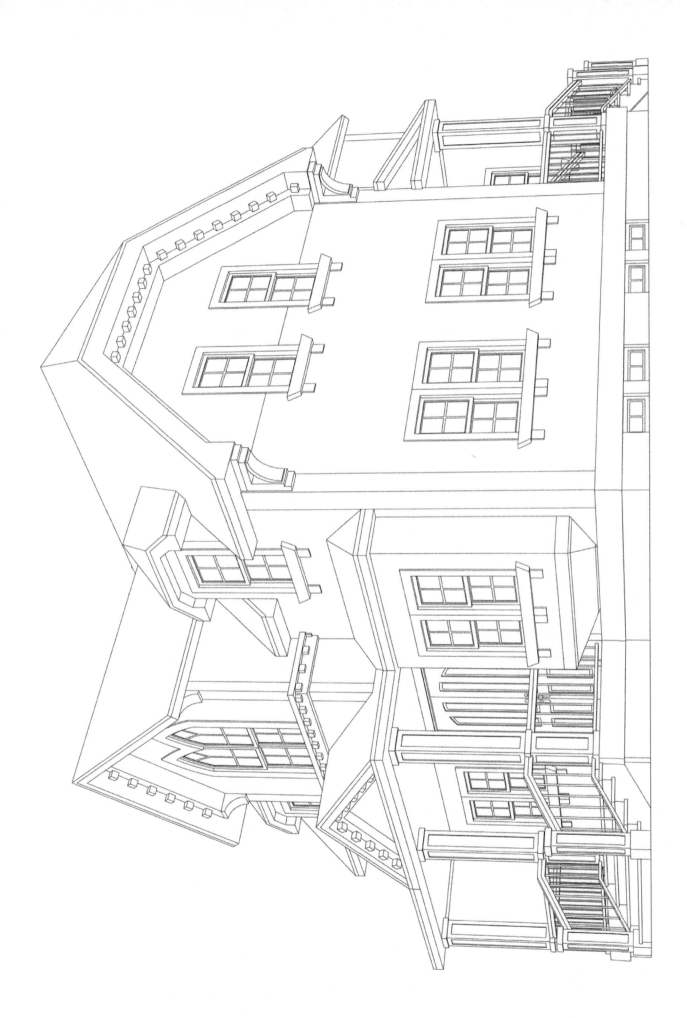

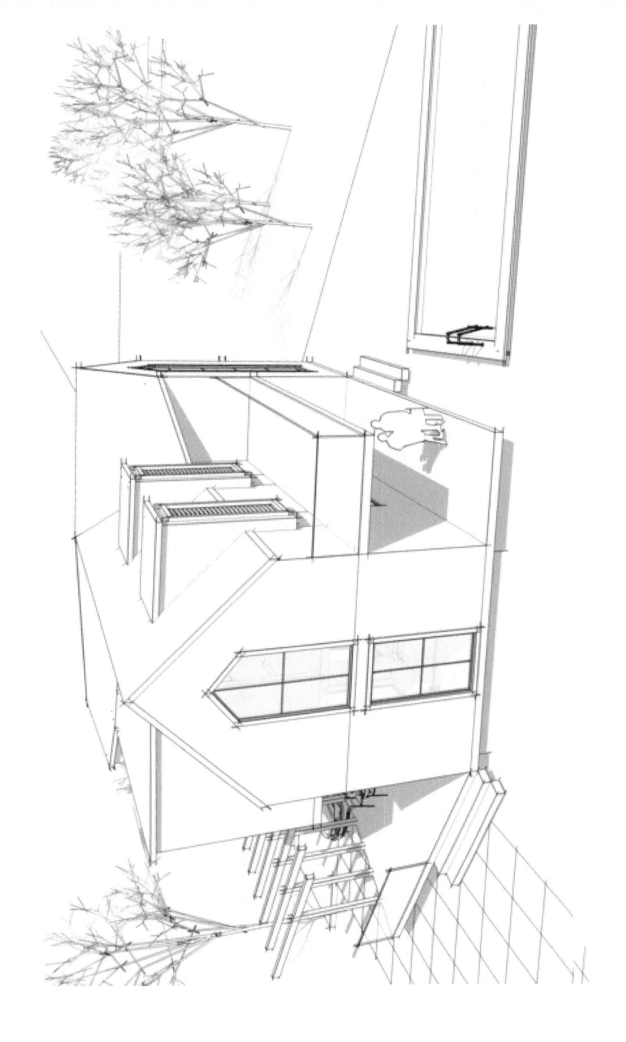

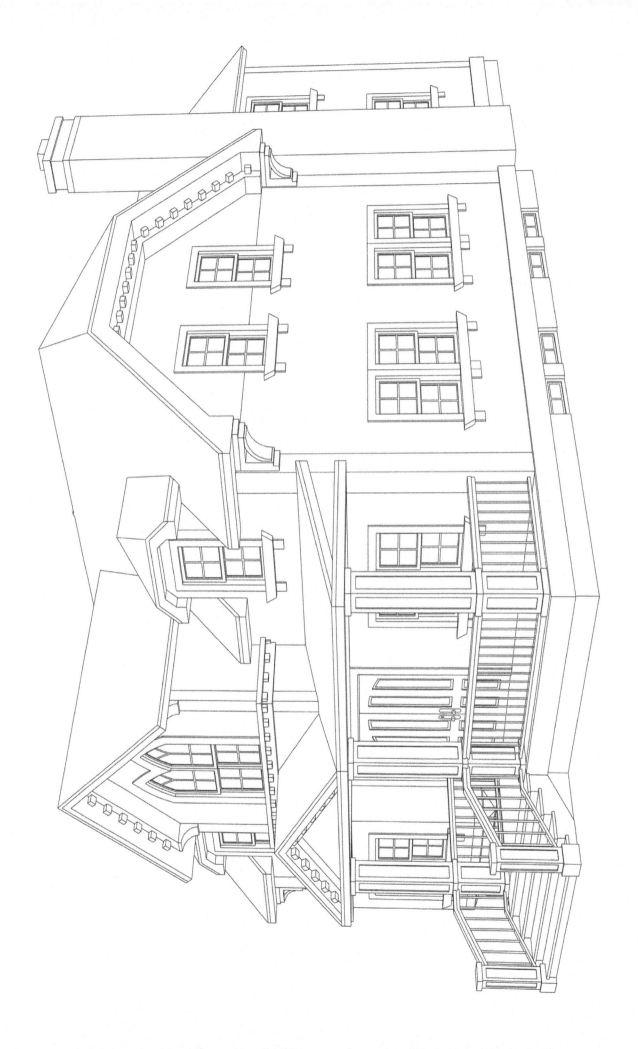

Thank you for coloring with us

Get more interior design coloring books:

LIVING ROOMS &
SPACE DESIGN SKETCHES

COLORING BOOK FOR ADULTS

RACHEL MINTZ

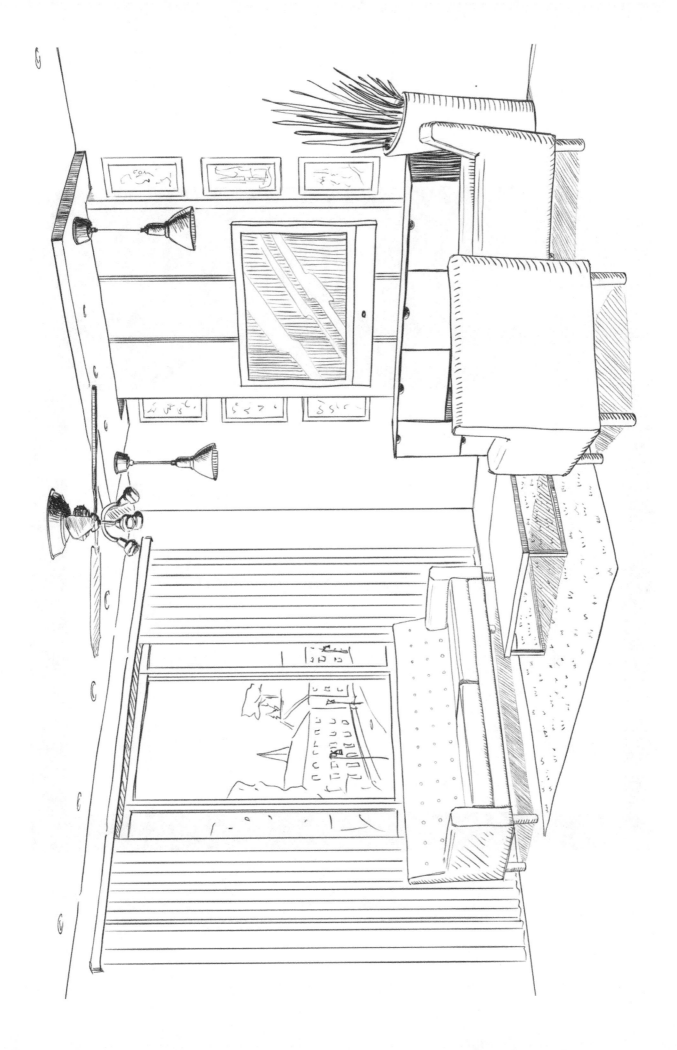

NEW interior design Coloring book at Amazon:

KITCHENS & HOME

SPACE DESIGN SKETCHES

COLORING BOOK FOR ADULTS

RACHEL MINTZ

Made in the USA
Las Vegas, NV
12 December 2023